# What do you know about ?
# SCIENCE and TECHNOLOGY
## Over 101 Questions and ANSWERS

Written by
Ian Graham & Andrew Langley

Vineyard
BOOKS

Photo Credits
p.31 Hank Morgan/Science Photo Library.


Planned and produced by
Andromeda Oxford Limited
11-15 The Vineyard
Abingdon
Oxon OX14 3PX

ISBN 1 86199 030 8

Printed in Singapore

# CONTENTS

# STARS & GALAXIES

**Q** What is a constellation?

**A** A constellation is a group of stars. Ancient astronomers gave many of them names, because they thought their patterns in the night sky made shapes which reminded them of things such as animals and gods. Many constellations are visible on a clear night. Some of these are shown below. There are 88 constellations.

**Q** What is a solar eclipse?

**A** As the Earth orbits the Sun, and the Moon orbits the Earth, all three sometimes line up. A solar eclipse (above) occurs when the Moon passes in front of the Sun and blocks out its light.

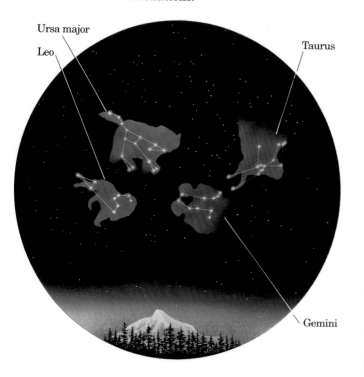

Ursa major

Leo

Taurus

Gemini

**Q** What shape is the Milky Way?

**A** The Sun is one of a hundred thousand million stars that form a galaxy called the Milky Way. If we could look at the Milky Way from the outside, it would look like a glowing ball surrounded by a thin disc of curling arms. We live in one of the galaxy's arms. Because of its shape, the Milky Way is called a spiral galaxy.

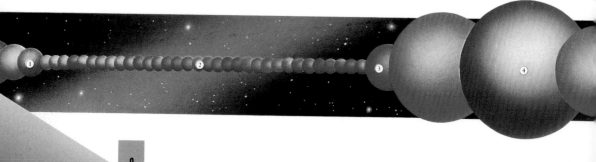

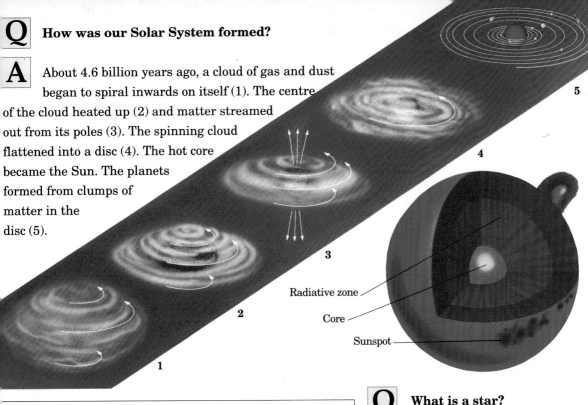

**Q**  How was our Solar System formed?

**A**  About 4.6 billion years ago, a cloud of gas and dust began to spiral inwards on itself (1). The centre of the cloud heated up (2) and matter streamed out from its poles (3). The spinning cloud flattened into a disc (4). The hot core became the Sun. The planets formed from clumps of matter in the disc (5).

5

4

3

2

1

Radiative zone

Core

Sunspot

**Q**  What is a star?

**A**  A star, like the Sun (above), is a large, burning ball of gases. The gas is mostly hydrogen. The hydrogen atoms are packed so tightly in the star's core that they join together to make a different gas, helium. This process, called nuclear fusion, releases an enormous amount of energy, which produces heat and light.

**Q**  Where did the galaxies come from?

**A**  The Universe began about 15 thousand million years ago in an explosion called The Big Bang. Matter formed in the explosion collected together in clouds. The clouds collapsed inwards and formed clumps of stars, the galaxies, spinning through space.

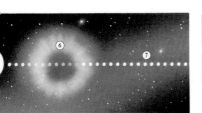

**Q**  How does a star die?

**A**  When a star like the Sun (left) burns all of its hydrogen, it begins to die. It puffs up to form a star called a red giant. It then shrinks and cools to become a tiny white dwarf star.

# EXPLORING SPACE

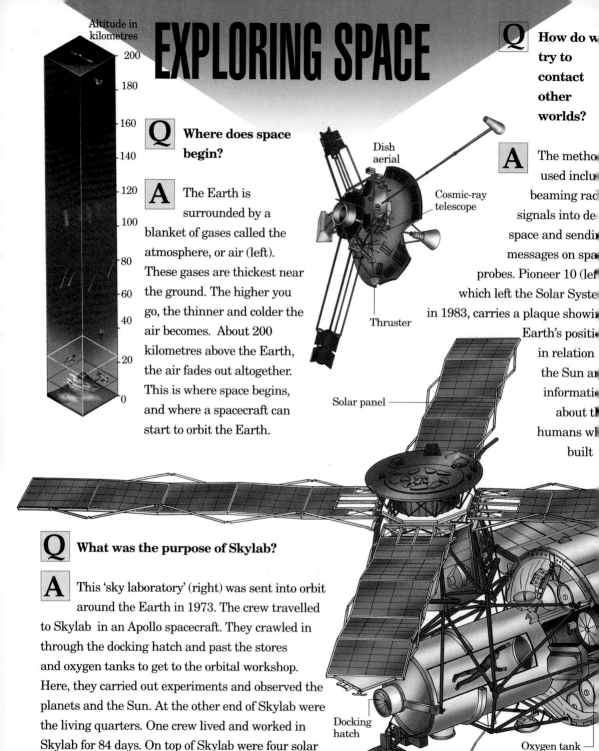

Altitude in kilometres

200
180
160
140
120
100
80
60
40
20
0

## Q Where does space begin?

**A** The Earth is surrounded by a blanket of gases called the atmosphere, or air (left). These gases are thickest near the ground. The higher you go, the thinner and colder the air becomes. About 200 kilometres above the Earth, the air fades out altogether. This is where space begins, and where a spacecraft can start to orbit the Earth.

Dish aerial

Cosmic-ray telescope

Thruster

## Q How do w try to contact other worlds?

**A** The metho used inclu beaming rad signals into de space and sendi messages on spa probes. Pioneer 10 (lef which left the Solar Syste in 1983, carries a plaque showi Earth's positi in relation the Sun a informati about tl humans wl built

Solar panel

## Q What was the purpose of Skylab?

**A** This 'sky laboratory' (right) was sent into orbit around the Earth in 1973. The crew travelled to Skylab in an Apollo spacecraft. They crawled in through the docking hatch and past the stores and oxygen tanks to get to the orbital workshop. Here, they carried out experiments and observed the planets and the Sun. At the other end of Skylab were the living quarters. One crew lived and worked in Skylab for 84 days. On top of Skylab were four solar panels which made power from sunlight.

Docking hatch

Oxygen tank

## Q  What is a space telescope?

**A** Earth telescopes have to look into space through the dust and moisture the atmosphere. Telescopes out in space ve a much clearer view. The Hubble lescope (below) orbits the Earth.

## Q  Which was the first space station?

**A** Salyut 1 (below) was the first ever space station. It was launched into orbit by the Russians in 1971. The crew was brought to Salyut 1 by a Soyuz spacecraft. Salyut's first crew spent 23 days on board – a record at the time.

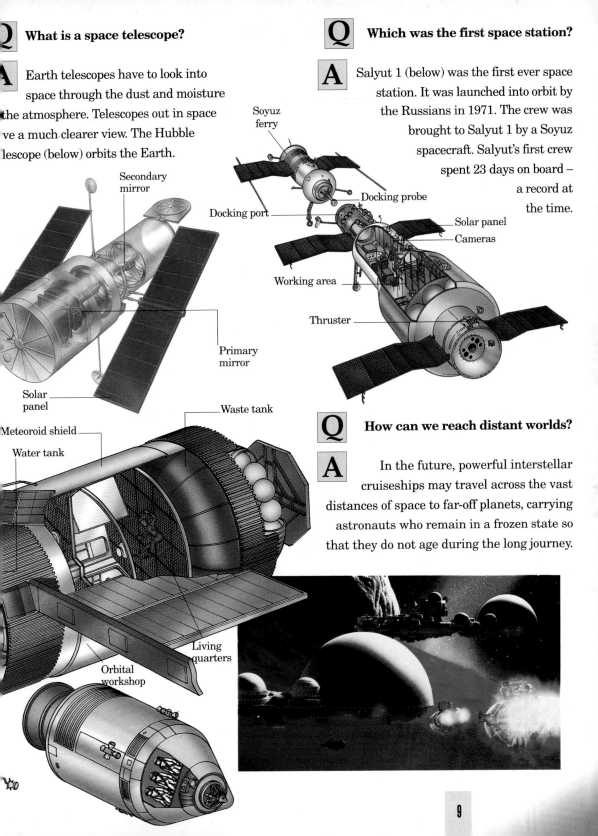

Secondary mirror

Docking port

Primary mirror

Solar panel

Soyuz ferry

Docking probe

Solar panel

Cameras

Working area

Thruster

Waste tank

Meteoroid shield

Water tank

Living quarters

Orbital workshop

## Q  How can we reach distant worlds?

**A** In the future, powerful interstellar cruiseships may travel across the vast distances of space to far-off planets, carrying astronauts who remain in a frozen state so that they do not age during the long journey.

# MAN IN SPACE

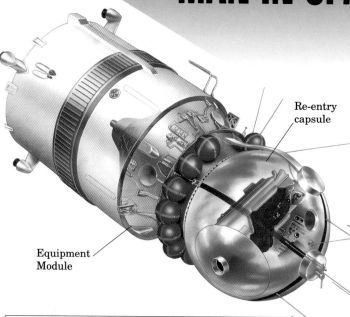

Re-entry capsule

Equipment Module

**Q** Who was the first man space?

**A** The first man in space wa Yuri Gagarin from the former Soviet Union. On April 1 1961, his tiny Vostok space caps (left), only 2.3 metres across, ma one orbit of the Earth. The spherical capsule then separated from its Equipment Module and rocket before plunging back into the Earth's atmosphere and landing by parachute.

**Q** How did astronauts land on the Moon?

**A** Apollo astronauts travelled to the Moon in a spacecraft made from three modules linked together. They lived in the cone-shaped Command Module. A Service Module supplied it with oxygen and electric power. Once they were in orbit around the Moon, two of the three astronauts moved into the Lunar Module. They separated it from the rest of the spacecraft and landed on the Moon.

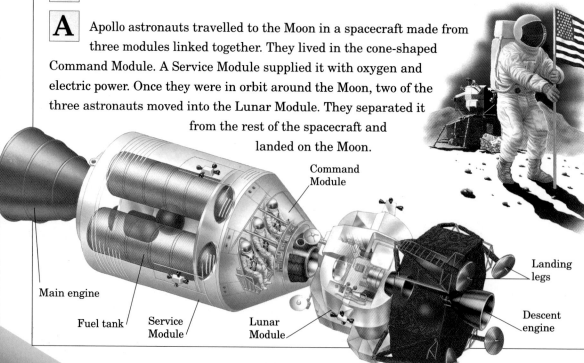

Command Module

Landing legs

Main engine

Descent engine

Fuel tank    Service Module    Lunar Module

## Q How do cosmonauts return to Earth?

**A** Before the Space Shuttle, all American manned spacecraft landed in the Pacific Ocean. Russian Soyuz spacecraft (below) are brought down on land. The small Re-entry Module descends through the atmosphere by parachute. Just before it touches the ground, rockets in the base of the spacecraft fire to cushion the landing.

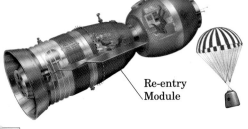

Re-entry Module

## Q How is a space station built?

**A** A space station is far too big to launch in one piece. Instead, it is launched in sections that have to be connected together in space. The Russian space station Mir (right) was launched in four pieces. The base unit was launched first in 1986. It was followed by three more modules that were linked to the base unit.

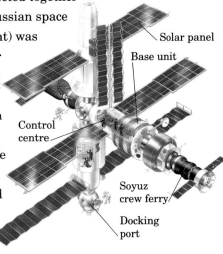

Solar panel

Base unit

Control centre

Soyuz crew ferry

Docking port

## Q How does the Space Shuttle take off?

**A** Six seconds before lift-off, three rocket engines in the Space Shuttle's tail fire. They burn fuel supplied by the large fuel tank underneath the spacecraft (below). Then the rocket boosters on each side of the fuel tank fire. Clamps holding the spacecraft down on the launch-pad are released and the Space Shuttle takes off.

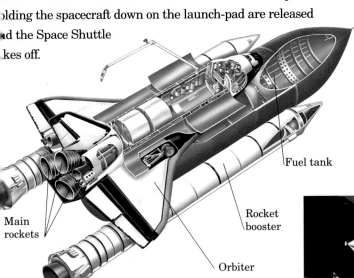

Fuel tank

Main rockets

Rocket booster

Orbiter

## Q What fuels might future spacecraft use?

**A** Future spacecraft will probably be powered by new types of engines instead of rockets. The ramscoop (below) collects hydrogen atoms from space in a large funnel and its engine fuses them together to release energy. The photon sail (bottom) is 'blown' through space by light from the Sun or lasers.

Hydrogen

Oxygen

**Water molecule**

**Oxygen atoms    Oxygen molecule**

## Q  What are molecules?

**A**   A molecule (above) is the
simplest part of a substance
that can take part in chemical
reactions. It is a group of two or more
atoms linked together. The atoms
may be the same or different. For
example, a molecule of water is made
of two hydrogen atoms linked to an
oxygen atom. An oxygen molecule is
made of two oxygen atoms linked
together.

## Q  What is the difference between a mixture and a compound?

**A**   If iron filings and sulphur (1) are
mixed together (2), there is no
chemical reaction and they can be
separated again by removing the
iron with a magnet (3). When iron
filings and sulphur are heated (4)
they combine and change into iron
sulphide, a compound.

## Q  What chemicals are used in fire extinguishers?

**A**   Carbon dioxide
extinguishers
send out a jet of carbon dioxide
gas. Dry powder extinguishers
blanket a fire with powder.
Soda-acid extinguishers (right)
mix sulphuric acid with sodium
carbonate, making carbon
dioxide gas which forces out a
jet of water.

Sodium
carbonat

Sulphuric acid

## Q  How do soaps and detergents work?

**A**   Soaps and detergents are made from long
molecules that are water-loving at one end
and grease-loving at the other end. When they go to
work on dirty cloth, they surround each
droplet of greasy dirt stuck to the
fibres of the cloth with their
grease-loving tails plugged int
the grease droplet (below). Th
coated droplet then floats off
the cloth into the water and
washed away.

Grease

Cloth

# Q How are chemicals made?

A The chemical industry makes chemicals by processing raw materials with heat, pressure and chemical reactions. Sulphuric acid is made from sulphur in a series of stages (right) that change sulphur into different compounds, ending with sulphuric acid.

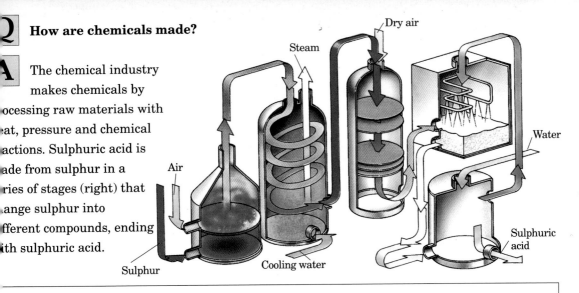

Dry air

Steam

Air

Water

Sulphur

Cooling water

Sulphuric acid

# Q What are crystals?

A Crystals are solid pieces of material with flat faces set at angles to each other. All crystals of the same substance have the same angles between their faces. Crystals form in this way because their atoms always lie in the same regular patterns. Salt, sugar and quartz are crystals. Minerals can sometimes be identified by the shape of their crystals.

# Q What is chemical analysis?

A Chemists use chemical analysis (right) to find out what an unknown substance contains. There are several methods. Volumetric analysis involves reactions in solutions. Gravimetric analysis involves weighing. In gas-liquid chromatography gas carries the sample through a column of moist powder. The sample separates into simpler compounds which are recorded on a chart as they leave the column.

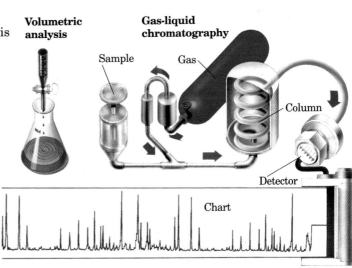

Volumetric analysis

Gas-liquid chromatography

Sample

Gas

Column

Detector

Chart

# MATERIALS

**Metal fuselage**

**Rubber tyres**

**Pottery vase**

**Glass flask**

**Plastic biro**

**Wood**

## Q What are materials?

**A** Materials are what we use to make the things we need. The first people used natural materials such as rock, wood, plant fibres and animal bones and skins. Then they learned how to make new materials. They made clay pots and baked them at high temperatures to harden them. They discovered how to make iron, bronze, copper and other metals. Glass was being made as long as 5,000 years ago. Today, we use more materials than ever, including a wide range of plastics.

## Q What materials come from plants?

**A** People have used materials taken from plants since prehistoric times, and plants are still a very important source of materials today. Timber, resins, rubber, cotton, linen, dyes, essential oils and a wide range of medicines are still obtained from plants.

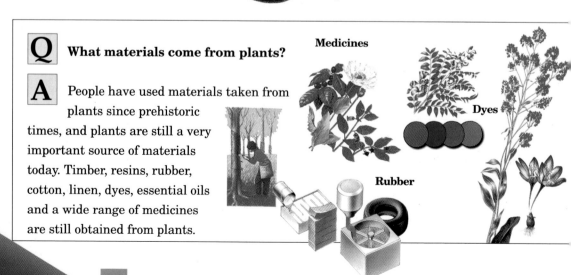

**Medicines**

**Dyes**

**Rubber**

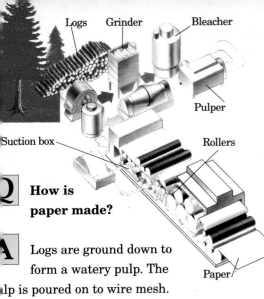

Logs  Grinder  Bleacher

Pulper

Suction box

Rollers

## Q How is paper made?

## A
Logs are ground down to form a watery pulp. The
Paper

pulp is poured on to wire mesh. Water is sucked and rolled out, leaving a thin film of paper. The process is continuous. Pulp is fed into one end of the machine (above) and paper comes out at the other end.

## Q What are composites?

## A
Composites are materials made by combining two or more materials. Many kinds of boats (above) are made by laying mats of glass fibres into a mould and then soaking the mats in liquid plastic. The plastic sets hard and is reinforced by the fibres to make a smooth, tough, lightweight hull.

## Q What do we get from crude oil?

## A
Crude oil is separated into materials ranging from bitumen for road-making to fuels such as petrol and gas. Crude oil is heated inside a tall fractionating tower (right). Gas and light fuels evaporate and collect near the top of the tower, leaving heavier oils and bitumen to settle at the bottom.

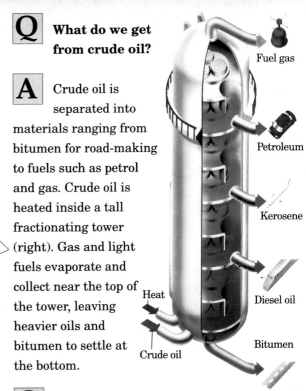

Fuel gas

Petroleum

Kerosene

Heat

Diesel oil

Crude oil

Bitumen

## Q How is plastic recycled?

## A
Waste plastic is loaded into a furnace (below) and heated. The gas given off is then separated in a distillation column. Wax and tar collect at the bottom, while lighter gases collect further up. Some of the gas is fed back to fuel the furnace.

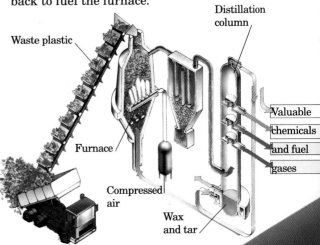

Distillation column

Waste plastic

Valuable chemicals and fuel gases

Furnace

Compressed air

Wax and tar

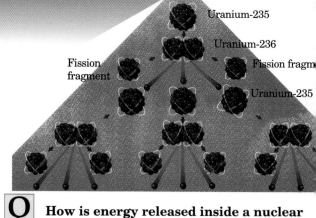

Slow-moving neutron

Uranium-235

Uranium-236

Fission fragment

Fission fragm

Uranium-235

## Q What is gravity?

**A** Gravity is the force that pulls everything to Earth. Galileo showed that gravity makes all objects fall equally fast. When he dropped a light ball and a heavy ball from the leaning Tower of Pisa (above), they hit the ground at the same instant.

## Q What is an Archimedes' Screw used for?

**A** The Archimedes' Screw (below) was invented by Archimedes in Ancient Greece. It is used for lifting water. One end of the screw is dipped into water. By turning the handle, the water is raised up inside the tube until it spills out of the top.

## Q How is energy released inside a nuclear reactor?

**A** A slow-moving neutron is made to hit an atom uranium-235 (above). It combines with the nucleus at the centre of the atom, forming uranium-236. This splits into two particles called fission fragments, releasing a burst of energy and three more neutrons, which split more uranium atoms.

## Q What forces act on an aeroplane in flight?

**A** Four forces act on an aeroplane. Its weight acts downwards. The thrust of its engines pushes it forwards. Lift created by its wings acts upwards. Drag tries to slow it down. Thrust must overcome drag, and lift must overcome weight, if a plane is to fly.

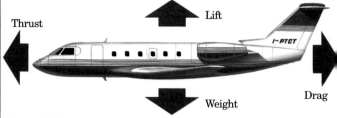

Lift

Thrust

Weight

Drag

## How does a space rocket work?

A rocket motor propels a rocket by burning fuel [mi]xed with an oxidiser. The [oxi]diser contains oxygen, which [is] necessary for burning. The [Ari]ane V rocket (below), burns [hy]drogen fuel with oxygen. The [ho]t gas produced rushes out of [the] motor nozzles, forcing the [roc]ket upwards.

el tank

oster
ket

idiser
[tan]k

cket
[mo]tor

[mo]tor
[no]zzle

## What is a force?

A force is something that changes an object's speed or direction. Forces always exist in pairs acting in opposite directions. When a rifle is fired (below right), the rifle kicks back as the bullet flies forwards. A heavier football player running faster applies a greater force than a lighter, slower player (below left).

## What is friction?

Friction is a force that stops surfaces sliding across each other easily. Sometimes friction is helpful. It allows our shoes to grip the ground. Without friction walking would be impossible. But friction can also be a problem because it wears out the moving parts of machines.

## How does a turbine work?

A turbine (right) is a machine that uses gas or liquid to make a shaft turn. Water hitting the buckets of a Pelton wheel drives the buckets round and turns the shaft. Wind spins the blades of a wind turbine. Wind and water turbines often drive electricity generators.

**Wind turbine**

Rotor blade

Generator

**Pelton wheel**

Water jet

Shaft

Buckets

# SOUND

Direction of wave →

## Q What is sound?

Rarefaction  Compression  Rarefaction

## A
Sound is a form of energy. Sound is made when something vibrates in air. The vibrations push against the surrounding air molecules, forming a sound wave. First the air molecules are squeezed (this is called compression), then they are stretched (this is called rarefaction). It is easiest to think of sound waves moving in the same way as a wave of energy moves along a coil of spring if one end is moved up and down (above).

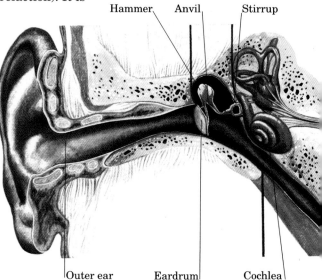

Hammer  Anvil  Stirrup

## Q How do we hear sounds?

## A
When sound waves reach us, the outer ear channels them inside the ear, where they make the eardrum vibrate. The vibrations are magnified 20 times by the hammer, anvil, and stirrup bones, causing liquid to vibrate inside a tube called the cochlea (right). Nerves in the cochlea pass messages to the brain, enabling us to recognise the sound.

Outer ear  Eardrum  Cochlea

## Q How fast does sound travel?

## A
Sound travels through solids, liquids and gases at different speeds. Its speed depends on the density the material. It travels faster through dense materials li steel than through less dense materials like air (below).

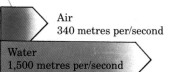

Air
340 metres per/second

Water
1,500 metres per/second

Concrete
5,000 metres per/second

Steel
6,000 metres per/second

## Q How is loudness measured?

## A Loudness depends on the amount of energy carried by a sound wave. The loudness of sound is measured in decibels (dB). Sounds louder than 120dB can damage the ears. Sounds louder than 130dB cause pain. Some animals, like bats, make sounds that we cannot hear at all (below).

ibels 140    Pain threshold

130

100

70

40

0

## Q Why does the sound of a racing car engine change as it drives past us?

## A As the racing car (right) approaches, the sound waves in front of it get squashed together. These short sound waves make the engine's noise sound high pitched. As the car moves past, the sound waves become stretched out behind it. The longer waves make the engine's note sound lower.

## Q How does sound travel down telephone wires?

Magnet

## A A carbon block in the mouthpiece converts the sound pressure waves of the caller's voice into electrical signals. These flow along wires (below) to the telephone at the other end. The magnet in the earpiece converts the signals back into sound pressure waves.

Carbon
block

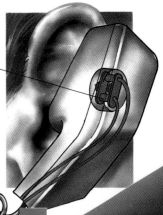

# ELECTRICITY & MAGNETISM

## Q How do electric vehicles work?

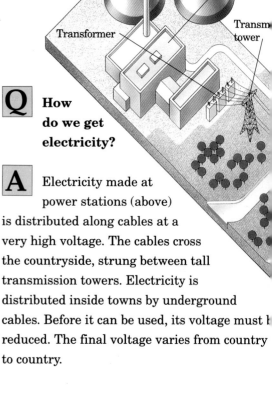

**A** An electric car (above) works by using electricity stored in batteries to power an electric motor connected to the car's wheels. Electric trains are supplied with electricity from wires above the track or a third rail beside the track. It powers electric motors that turn the wheels.

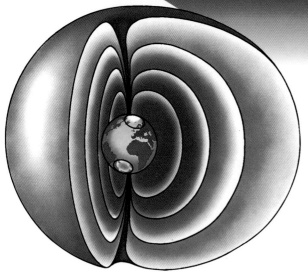

## Q What is a magnetic field?

**A** A magnetic field is a region of forces that exists around a magnet. The field can be drawn as a series of curved lines, called lines of force, joining the magnet's north and south poles. The Earth behaves like a magnet. Its magnetic field (above), caused by electric currents inside the liquid part of its core, stretches thousands of kilometres into space.

## Q How are magnets made?

**A** An iron bar contains molecular magnets pointing in all directions. If the bar is placed inside a coil carrying an electric current, the molecular magnets line up with the coil's magnetic field. The bar has now become a magnet (right).

Power statio

Transformer

Transm tower

## Q How do we get electricity?

**A** Electricity made at power stations (above) is distributed along cables at a very high voltage. The cables cross the countryside, strung between tall transmission towers. Electricity is distributed inside towns by underground cables. Before it can be used, its voltage must be reduced. The final voltage varies from country to country.

## Q How do electric motors work?

## A An electric motor is made of a coil of wire inside a
magnet. The coil is free to turn. When an electric
current flows through the coil, it magnetises the coil.
This magnetic field pushes against the magnetic field
produced by the surrounding magnet and this makes the
coil spin.

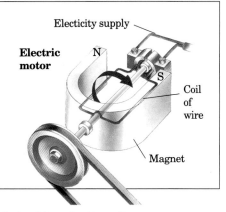

Electicity supply

**Electric motor**

N

S

Coil of wire

Magnet

## Q How does a doorbell work?

## A When the bell push (below) is
pressed, the coil becomes
agnetised. The iron rod shoots out of the
il and strikes the short chime. When the
ll push is released, the rod swings back
to the coil and hits
e long chime.

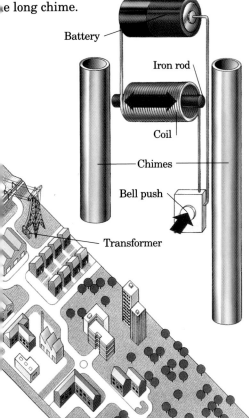

Battery

Iron rod

Coil

Chimes

Bell push

Transformer

## Q What is inside a battery?

## A Cars and trucks use a type of battery called
an accumulator (below). It contains flat
plates of lead and lead oxide dipped in sulphuric
acid. When the battery is connected to a circuit, a
chemical reaction between the plates and the acid
makes an electric current flow round the circuit.
An accumulator is recharged by passing an electric
current through it.

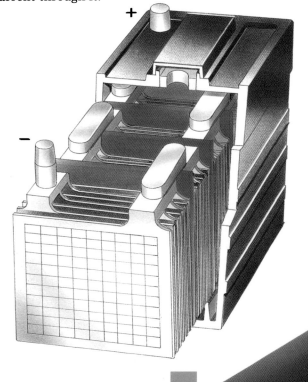

+

−

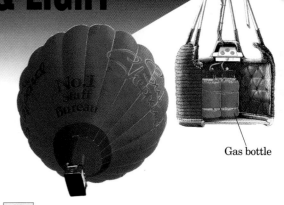

Gas burr

Gas bottle

**Q** What is light?

**A** Light is a form of energy. It is composed of waves of electric and magnetic vibrations which our eyes can detect. The different colours (below) are produced by light waves of different lengths. We are unable to see waves shorter than blue light and longer than red.

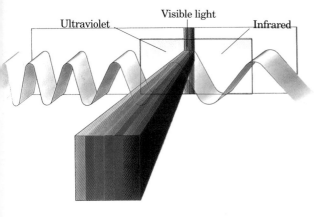

Ultraviolet    Visible light    Infrared

**Q** How does a hot air balloon rise?

**A** A gas burner supplied by gas from bottle the balloon's basket (above) heats the air inside the balloon. As the air warms up, it expar The thinner air inside the balloon is lighter thar the surrounding air, so the balloon floats upward

**Q** How does a laser work?

**A** Light is normally composed of differer wavelengths (colours) mixed at randor A laser produces an intense beam of high-energy light in which all the light is of the same wavelength. The process is started by a electric current or a flash of light from a flasl tube which causes a gas or ruby ro (below) to send out the laser beam.

**Q** How fast does light travel?

**A** The speed of light is 300,000 km/s, faster than anything else in the universe. Light takes roughly 8.5 minutes to travel from the Sun (below) to the Earth. Looking at distant objects allows us to look back in time. When we look at a remote galaxy, we see it as it was when the light left it.

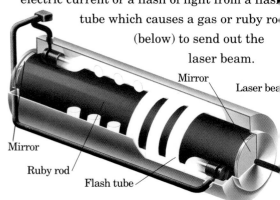

Mirror

Laser bea

Mirror

Ruby rod

Flash tube

## Q What are thermals?

## A Birds can often be seen gliding in tight circles, being carried upwards by rising columns of air called thermals (right). ...round heated by the Sun warms the air above it. The warm air ...ses, sucking cool air in below it. That, too, is warmed and ...ses up. Glider pilots use thermals. They circle ...d climb inside one thermal, then glide to the ...xt (below).

Bird's flight path

Thermal

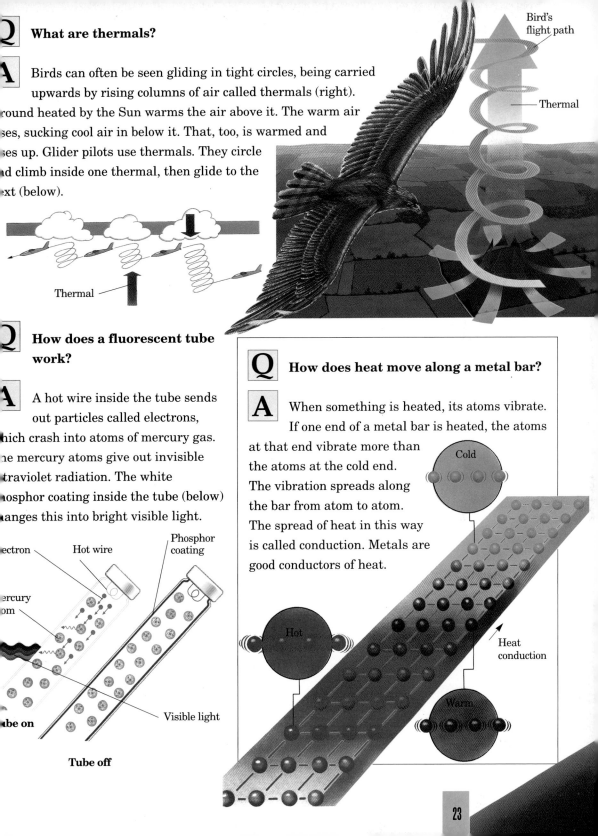

Thermal

## Q How does a fluorescent tube work?

## A A hot wire inside the tube sends out particles called electrons, ...hich crash into atoms of mercury gas. ...e mercury atoms give out invisible ...traviolet radiation. The white ...osphor coating inside the tube (below) ...anges this into bright visible light.

...ectron    Hot wire    Phosphor coating

...ercury ...om

...be on    Visible light

**Tube off**

## Q How does heat move along a metal bar?

## A When something is heated, its atoms vibrate. If one end of a metal bar is heated, the atoms at that end vibrate more than the atoms at the cold end. The vibration spreads along the bar from atom to atom. The spread of heat in this way is called conduction. Metals are good conductors of heat.

Cold

Hot

Warm

Heat conduction

# SHIPS

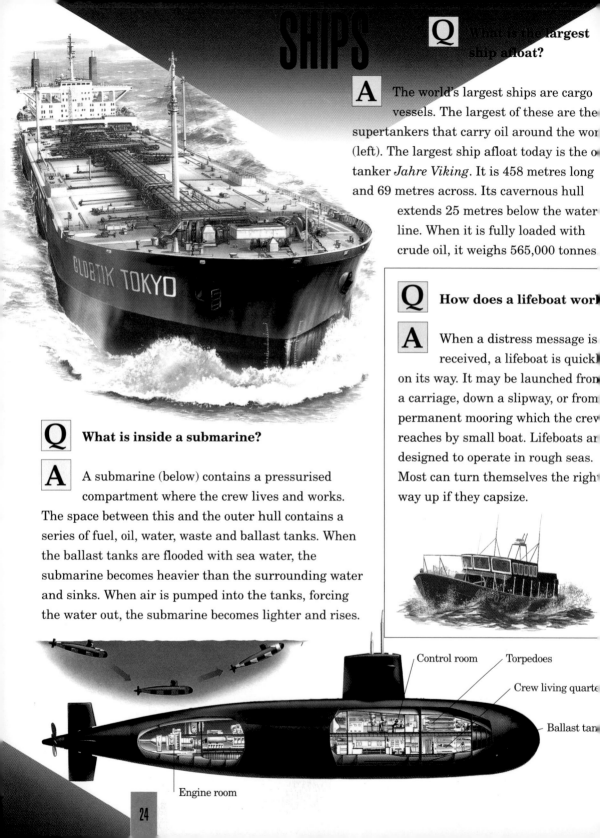

**Q** What is the largest ship afloat?

**A** The world's largest ships are cargo vessels. The largest of these are the supertankers that carry oil around the wor (left). The largest ship afloat today is the o tanker *Jahre Viking*. It is 458 metres long and 69 metres across. Its cavernous hull extends 25 metres below the water line. When it is fully loaded with crude oil, it weighs 565,000 tonnes

**Q** How does a lifeboat worl

**A** When a distress message is received, a lifeboat is quickl on its way. It may be launched from a carriage, down a slipway, or from permanent mooring which the crew reaches by small boat. Lifeboats ar designed to operate in rough seas. Most can turn themselves the right way up if they capsize.

**Q** What is inside a submarine?

**A** A submarine (below) contains a pressurised compartment where the crew lives and works. The space between this and the outer hull contains a series of fuel, oil, water, waste and ballast tanks. When the ballast tanks are flooded with sea water, the submarine becomes heavier than the surrounding water and sinks. When air is pumped into the tanks, forcing the water out, the submarine becomes lighter and rises.

GLOBTIK TOKYO

Control room    Torpedoes

Crew living quarte

Ballast tan

Engine room

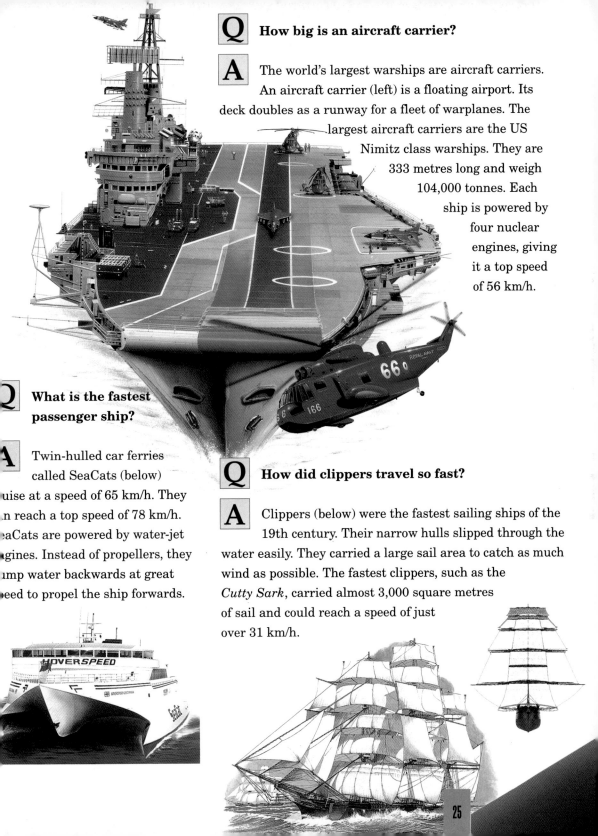

**Q** How big is an aircraft carrier?

**A** The world's largest warships are aircraft carriers. An aircraft carrier (left) is a floating airport. Its deck doubles as a runway for a fleet of warplanes. The largest aircraft carriers are the US Nimitz class warships. They are 333 metres long and weigh 104,000 tonnes. Each ship is powered by four nuclear engines, giving it a top speed of 56 km/h.

**Q** What is the fastest passenger ship?

**A** Twin-hulled car ferries called SeaCats (below) cruise at a speed of 65 km/h. They can reach a top speed of 78 km/h. SeaCats are powered by water-jet engines. Instead of propellers, they pump water backwards at great speed to propel the ship forwards.

**Q** How did clippers travel so fast?

**A** Clippers (below) were the fastest sailing ships of the 19th century. Their narrow hulls slipped through the water easily. They carried a large sail area to catch as much wind as possible. The fastest clippers, such as the *Cutty Sark*, carried almost 3,000 square metres of sail and could reach a speed of just over 31 km/h.

25

# FLIGHT

**Q** How does an aeroplane stay in the air?

**A** Aeroplanes (left) can fly because of the shape of their wings. The top of the wing is more curved than the bottom. Air rushing over the top of the wings travels further and faster than the air flowing underneath. This produces lower air pressure above the wings than below them (below), causing the wings to lift.

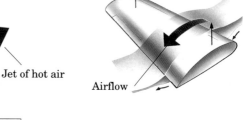

Jet of hot air

Airflow

**Q** What happens before take-off?

**A** An airliner (below) is carefully prepared for each flight. The passenger cabin is cleaned. Meals and luggage are loaded. The fuel tanks are filled. Engineers check the plane and the crew make their pre-flight checks.

Combustion chamber

Fan

**Q** How does a jet engine work?

**A** A large spinning fan at the front of the engine (above) sucks in air. The air is then compressed and heated by burning fuel in the combustion chamber. This makes the air expand quickly. A jet of hot air rushes out of the back of the engine and pushes the aeroplane forwards.

**Q** What did the first aeroplane look like?

**A** The first aeroplane, called *Flyer 1* (right), flew in 1903. [I]t was made from wood. It had two [wi]ngs covered with fabric, one [ab]ove the other, and the pilot lay [do]wn on the lower wing to fly it.

**Q** What is a Zeppelin?

**A** A Zeppelin (left) is a giant airship named after its inventor, Count Ferdinand von Zeppelin. The Zeppelins were built in Germany between 1900 and the 1930s. The biggest passenger-carrying Zeppelins were the *Graf Zeppelin* and the *Hindenberg*. They carried passengers across the Atlantic Ocean. Zeppelins could fly without wings because they were filled with hydrogen gas. This is lighter than air and made the airships float upwards.

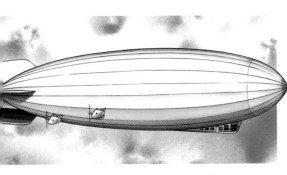

Hindenberg 245 metres

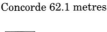 

Concorde 62.1 metres

**Q** Which aircraft can carry the largest cargo?

**A** The Airbus Super Transporter A300-600ST Beluga has the largest cargo hold of any aircraft. It can carry up to 45 tonnes of cargo in a hold that is 37 metres long and up to 7.4 metres wide. Belugas are built from Airbus A300 airliners. They replace the Super Guppy transporter (below). The Super Guppies were built to transport parts of the giant Saturn 5 moon rockets.

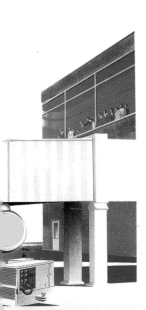

**AIRBUS SKYLINK**

F-BTGV

1

**Q** How are heavy loads carried by road?

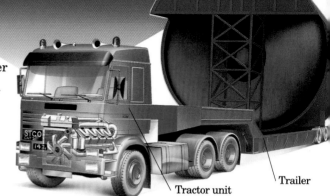

**A** The largest and heaviest loads are carried on a special low trailer pulled by a powerful tractor unit (right). This vehicle has six axles to spread the load. The tractor unit has six sets of wheels. Four of them are driven by the engine to give maximum power.

Trailer

Tractor unit

**Q** How does a refrigeration truck keep its cargo cold?

**A** Cargoes that have to be kept cold are transported in a refrigerated truck (below). The insulated trailer has a refrigeration unit on the front. Liquid coolant flows through pipes in the trailer and absorbs heat from the cargo. The coolant returns to the refrigeration unit and gives up its heat to the outside air. It is then compressed to turn it back into a cold liquid and re-circulated through the trailer.

Refrigeration unit

**Q** Which were the largest ever steam trains?

**A** The largest steam locomotives ever built were five giants called Big Boys. They were built in the 1940s for the US Union Pacific Railroad. The locomotive and its coal tender (right) were almost 40 metres long, 3 metres wide and 5 metres high. They each weighed 600 tonnes. They pulled up to 4,000 tonnes of freight in the Rocky Mountains.

## Q  Can the Sun power vehicles?

## A  Sunshine can be turned into electricity by solar cells. A vehicle covered with solar cells can produce enough electricity to drive an electric motor. A solar-powered bicycle crossed Australia at an average speed of 50 km/h. The fastest solar-powered car, Sunraycer, was capable of a top speed of 78 km/h.

## Q  What is the fastest train?

## A  The world's fastest train in service today is the French TGV (Train à Grande Vitesse) Atlantique. The first of these high-speed electric trains was introduced in 1981. On May 18, 1990 a TGV Atlantique train (right) reached the record-breaking speed of 515 km/h between Courtalain and Tours. In everyday passenger service, TGV Atlantiques normally travel at up to 300 km/h.

## Q  What is a supercar?

## A  Supercars are the super saloons and super sports models of the car world. They are fast, powerful and very expensive. The Ferrari F40 (right) is certainly a supercar. One of the world's fastest production cars, it can reach a top speed of 325 km/h. One special feature is that the engine is behind the driver.

# COMPUTERS

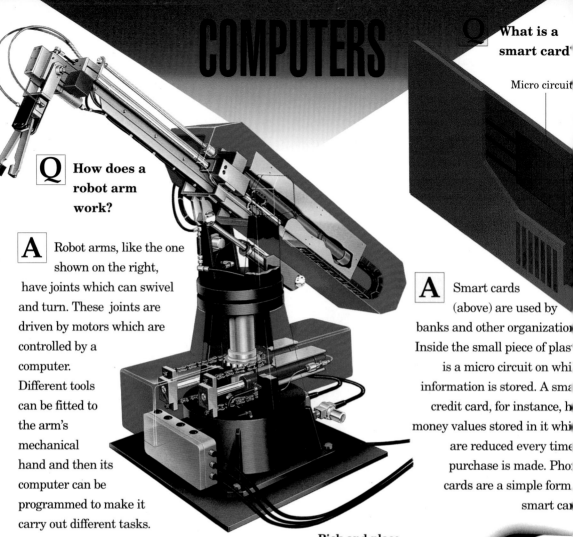

Micro circuit

**Q How does a robot arm work?**

**A** Robot arms, like the one shown on the right, have joints which can swivel and turn. These joints are driven by motors which are controlled by a computer. Different tools can be fitted to the arm's mechanical hand and then its computer can be programmed to make it carry out different tasks.

**A** Smart cards (above) are used by banks and other organization Inside the small piece of plas is a micro circuit on whi information is stored. A sma credit card, for instance, h money values stored in it whi are reduced every time purchase is made. Pho cards are a simple form smart ca

Pick-and-place robot

**Q What is virtual reality?**

**A** Virtual reality is a computerized fantasy world that seems like the real thing. To enter it, the user wears a helmet with a computer screen inside (right). As the user moves his/her head, different parts of the 'world' appear within the screen. In some virtual reality programs the user moves a joystick to make the images move on the screen. Sometimes sensors attached to the body enable the user to 'touch' things. The science of virtual reality is still at an early stage. It takes powerful computers to run even a simple program. Simulators used to train aircraft pilots and tank commanders use a form of virtual reality.

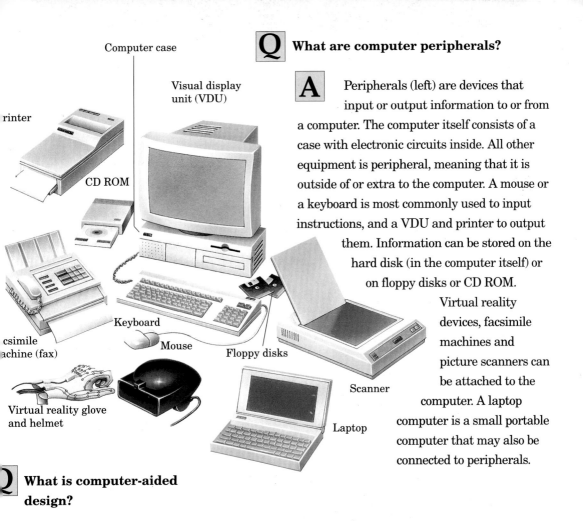

Computer case

Visual display unit (VDU)

rinter

CD ROM

csimile achine (fax)

Keyboard

Mouse

Floppy disks

Virtual reality glove and helmet

Scanner

Laptop

## Q What are computer peripherals?

**A** Peripherals (left) are devices that input or output information to or from a computer. The computer itself consists of a case with electronic circuits inside. All other equipment is peripheral, meaning that it is outside of or extra to the computer. A mouse or a keyboard is most commonly used to input instructions, and a VDU and printer to output them. Information can be stored on the hard disk (in the computer itself) or on floppy disks or CD ROM. Virtual reality devices, facsimile machines and picture scanners can be attached to the computer. A laptop computer is a small portable computer that may also be connected to peripherals.

## What is computer-aided design?

**A** Computer-aided design (CAD) is often used in industry. Details of a w product design are fed into a computer. e computer displays a model that signers can look at from all angles. They n test out new ideas on the model. For stance, the addition of a more powerful gine may require wider tyres. Here ght) a computer model is being used to st air flow over a car design. This shows at the addition of a small spoiler on the ar of the car will give better road holding.

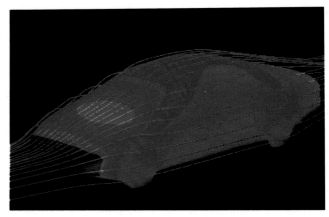

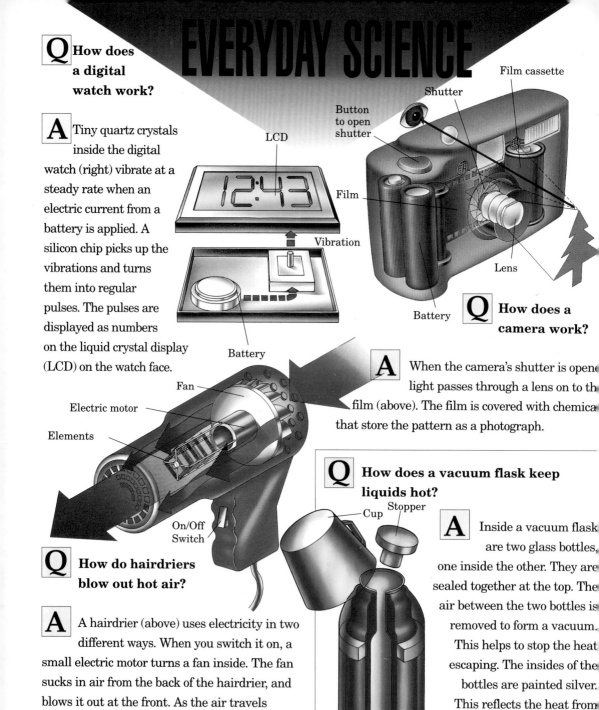

## Q How does a digital watch work?

**A** Tiny quartz crystals inside the digital watch (right) vibrate at a steady rate when an electric current from a battery is applied. A silicon chip picks up the vibrations and turns them into regular pulses. The pulses are displayed as numbers on the liquid crystal display (LCD) on the watch face.

LCD

Film

Vibration

Battery

## Q How does a camera work?

**A** When the camera's shutter is opened, light passes through a lens on to the film (above). The film is covered with chemicals that store the pattern as a photograph.

Film cassette

Shutter

Button to open shutter

Lens

Battery

## Q How do hairdriers blow out hot air?

Fan

Electric motor

Elements

On/Off Switch

**A** A hairdrier (above) uses electricity in two different ways. When you switch it on, a small electric motor turns a fan inside. The fan sucks in air from the back of the hairdrier, and blows it out at the front. As the air travels through the hairdrier, it passes over a set of wire coils called elements. These are heated by the electricity, warming the air as it passes.

## Q How does a vacuum flask keep liquids hot?

Cup

Stopper

**A** Inside a vacuum flask are two glass bottles, one inside the other. They are sealed together at the top. The air between the two bottles is removed to form a vacuum. This helps to stop the heat escaping. The insides of the bottles are painted silver. This reflects the heat from the liquid inside the flask.

Vacuum

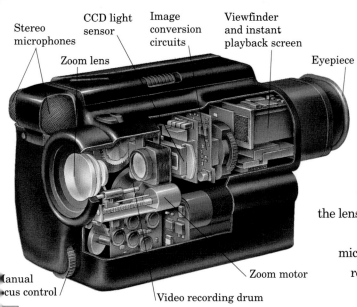

Stereo microphones
CCD light sensor
Image conversion circuits
Viewfinder and instant playback screen
Zoom lens
Eyepiece
Manual focus control
Zoom motor
Video recording drum

**Q** What is inside a video camera?

**A** Inside a video camera, a single charge coupled device (CCD) chip converts the image formed by the lens into a colour video signal, which is recorded onto video tape. An infrared beam focuses the lens automatically, or the user can select manual focus. At the same time the microphones pick up the sound, which is recorded on the edge of the video tape.

## Why do bicycles have gears?

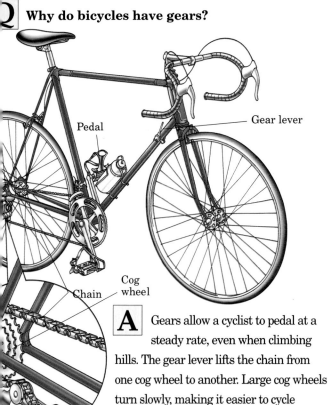

Gear lever
Pedal
Cog wheel
Chain

**A** Gears allow a cyclist to pedal at a steady rate, even when climbing hills. The gear lever lifts the chain from one cog wheel to another. Large cog wheels turn slowly, making it easier to cycle uphill. Small cog wheels turn quickly, making it easier to pedal downhill.

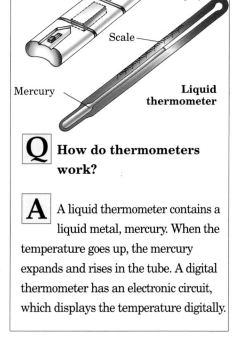

Digital thermometer
Digital display
Scale
Mercury
**Liquid thermometer**

**Q** How do thermometers work?

**A** A liquid thermometer contains a liquid metal, mercury. When the temperature goes up, the mercury expands and rises in the tube. A digital thermometer has an electronic circuit, which displays the temperature digitally.

# MACHINES

**Q** When was the first locomotive invented?

**A** On February 21, 1804
Richard Trevithick
demonstrated his latest invention at the
Penydarren mining railway in Wales. It was the world's
first railway locomotive (right). It made a journey of
16 kilometres in four hours pulling ten tonnes of
iron on which 70 men sat.

**Q** What is a bulldozer?

**A** A bulldozer is a machine used mainly on
building sites to shift earth. It has
caterpillar tracks to grip soft ground and a blade
at the front that can be raised or lowered. To
scrape the ground level, the bulldozer drives
forwards with the blade lowered.

**Q** How does a hovercraft work?

Air    Fan

**A** A hovercraft (below) travels over land and water by floating
on top of a cushion of air. Powerful fans inside the hovercraft
suck air down
underneath it. A
flexible rubber skirt
around the edge of the
hovercraft holds the air
in as the craft rises.
Propellers above
the deck spin
round to push the
hovercraft forward.

Propeller

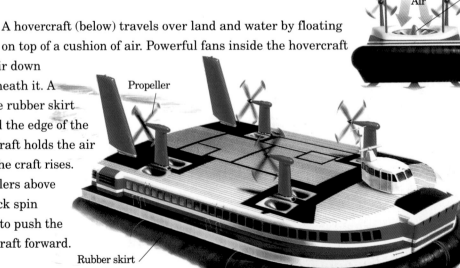

Rubber skirt

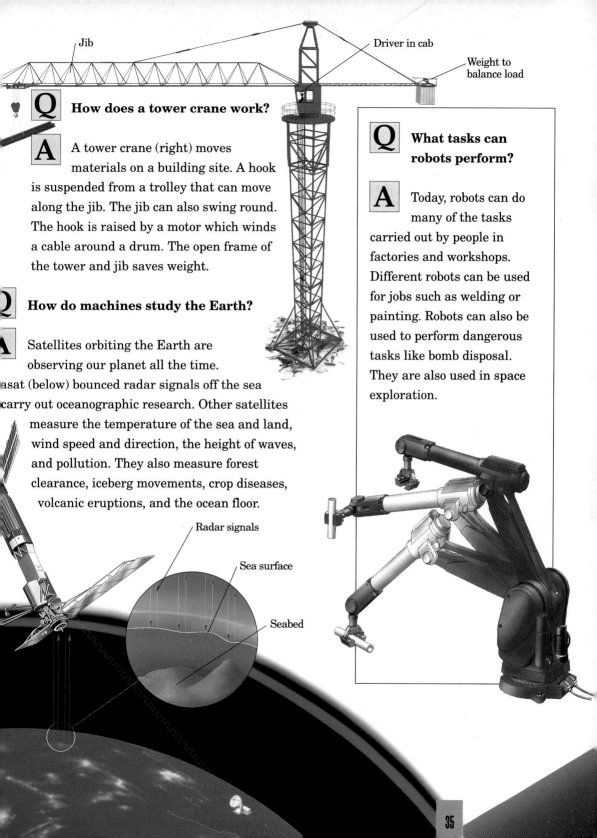

Jib

Driver in cab

Weight to balance load

## Q How does a tower crane work?

**A** A tower crane (right) moves materials on a building site. A hook is suspended from a trolley that can move along the jib. The jib can also swing round. The hook is raised by a motor which winds a cable around a drum. The open frame of the tower and jib saves weight.

## Q How do machines study the Earth?

**A** Satellites orbiting the Earth are observing our planet all the time. ...asat (below) bounced radar signals off the sea ...carry out oceanographic research. Other satellites measure the temperature of the sea and land, wind speed and direction, the height of waves, and pollution. They also measure forest clearance, iceberg movements, crop diseases, volcanic eruptions, and the ocean floor.

Radar signals

Sea surface

Seabed

## Q What tasks can robots perform?

**A** Today, robots can do many of the tasks carried out by people in factories and workshops. Different robots can be used for jobs such as welding or painting. Robots can also be used to perform dangerous tasks like bomb disposal. They are also used in space exploration.

# STRUCTURES

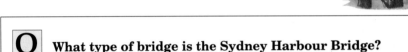

**Q** How long did it take to build the Great Pyramid?

**A** The Great Pyramid was built as a tomb for King Khufu, also called Cheops. It is at Giza, in Egypt. Work began in about 2,575 BC. It took thousands of people about 25 years to assemble it (right) from 2.3 million blocks of stone. It weighs over 6 million tonnes and is today 138 metres high. The Great Pyramid was the tallest building in the world for 4,000 years.

Buria
cham

**Q** What type of bridge is the Sydney Harbour Bridge?

**A** The Sydney Harbour Bridge in Australia is a steel arch bridge spanning 503 metres. It is not the longest steel arch, but it is the widest. It carries two railway tracks, eight traffic lanes, a cycle track and a footpath. It was opened in 1932.

**Q** What is the Eiffel Tower?

**A** The Eiffel Tower (right) is one of the most famous French landmarks. Designed by the engineer Alexandre-Gustave Eiffel, it was built in 1889 to celebrate the 100th anniversary of the French Revolution. It stands 300 metres high, and is a slender pyramid made from 7,000 tonnes of iron girders.

**Q** How is the space shuttle moved to its launch pad?

**A** The space shuttle (left) is prepared for launch inside a building at the Kennedy Space Center in Florida, USA. It is moved to the launch pad 6 kilometres away by the world's largest crawler transporter. This giant is 40 metres long and weighs 2,700 tonnes. It travels on four double caterpillar tracks. The tracks are moved by electric motors driven by generators powered by diesel engines.

**Q** What is an oil platform?

**A** Oil platforms are offshore drilling rigs which stand on the seabed. The tallest is the Auger platform in the Gulf of Mexico. It stands in 872 metres of water. The Gullfaks C platform (above) in the North Sea stands on concrete pillars and supports production equipment, loading derricks, and a helicopter pad.

**Q** How does a flood barrier work?

**A** The Thames Barrier (right) was opened in 1984 to protect London from flooding. It consists of eight gates each weighing 3,700 tonnes. They normally lie on the river bed. If there is any danger of flooding, the gates are rotated to raise them up against the flood water.

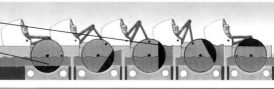

Gate raised

Gate lowered

# UNDERSEA EXPLORATION

**Q** How did early
diving suits work?

**A** Early diving
equipment made in
the 1600s and 1700s
worked by pumping air
down a hose from the
surface into a metal helmet
over the diver's head (right).
The pressure of the air inside
the helmet stopped water from
rising up inside.

**Q** How does a pressurised
diving suit work?

**A** A pressurised diving suit
(below) is supplied
with air pumped from the
surface through a hose. The
diver can alter the air
pressure inside the suit by
adjusting a valve in the
helmet. Heavy
metal boots
help to
keep the
diver weighted
down on the
seabed.

**Q** What is an atmospheric diving suit?

**A** An atmospheric diving suit (below) is a
watertight suit of armour used for the
deepest dives. The diver breathes air at
atmospheric pressure, which is
that of surface air. The heavy
metal suit with watertight
joints stops the huge water
pressure 300 metres below
the surface from
crushing it.

**Q** What is an aqualung?

**A** An aqualung (above) is a device which
enables divers to move around freely
under water without any connection with the
surface. The diver breathes air from tanks wor
on the back.

**Q** Why are shipwrecks explored?

**A** Sunken ships can tell us a lot about the sailors who sailed them and the world they lived in. The ship's timbers may be all that is left, but sometimes the divers who explore shipwrecks (right) find tools, guns and some of the sailors' belongings.

**Q** What animals have been found in the ocean depths?

**A** Light does not reach the bottom of the ocean. Many of the fish that live there make their own light. They catch smaller fish by dangling a glowing lure over their mouth. Smaller fish swim towards the lure and straight into the fish's mouth.

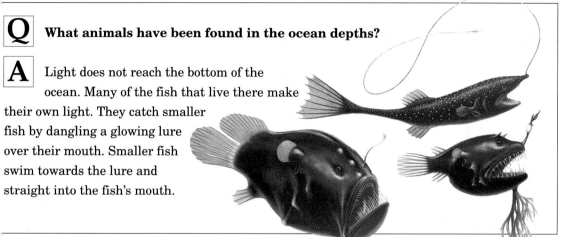

**Q** What was the deepest diving vessel?

**A** On January 23, 1960 the bathyscaphe *Trieste* (left) descended 10,916 metres into the deepest part of the Marianas Trench in the Pacific Ocean. No-one has dived deeper. *Trieste*'s crew of two were protected inside a thick metal sphere beneath a large float partly filled with petrol. When sea water flooded into the float, *Trieste* sank. To return to the surface, it dropped metal weights.

Propeller for manoeuvring

...er ...ast tank

...oyancy ...k

Crew compartment

TV camera

Mechanical arm

# SCIENCE OF LIFE

**Plant cell**

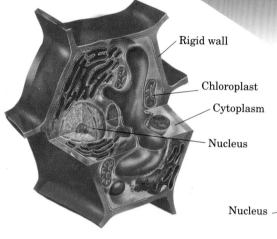

Rigid wall

Chloroplast

Cytoplasm

Nucleus

Non-rigid wall     **Animal cell**

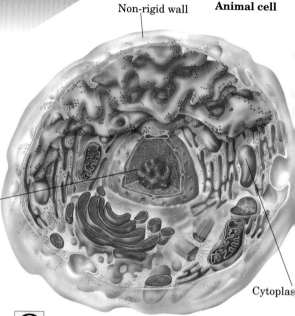

Nucleus

Cytoplas

## Q Why do animals of the same species fight?

**A** Animals fight others of their species for several reasons. They may be arguing over territory, or the right to be leader of their herd. Although many animals have powerful weapons, such as teeth, horns or claws, few are ever killed in these contests. These two klipspringer antelopes are jabbing at each other with their sharp horns.

## Q What is a cell?

**A** A cell (above) is the basic building block of almost every living thing. Plant cells have a rigid wall made from a material called cellulose. Animal cells do not have a rigid wall. Inside all cells is a fluid called cytoplasm, containing the nucleus and other small bodies. The nucleus is the cell's control centre. The chloroplasts in plant cells help trap the energy from sunlight. The energy is used to turn carbon dioxide and water into food for the plant.

**Q** How do plants make seeds?

Anther

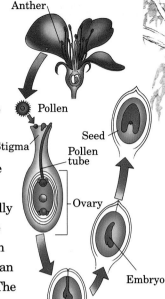

Pollen

Stigma

Seed

Pollen tube

Ovary

Embryo

**A** Plants have male and female parts at join together to make ds. A pollen grain vels from the male ther of one flower to the nale stigma of another ght). The pollen is usually rried by an insect or the nd. It fertilizes an egg in e ovary, which becomes an bryo and then a seed. The d will grow into a new plant.

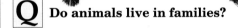

**Q** How do racing pigeons find their way home?

**A** Racing pigeons and many other species of birds probably use more than one way of navigating. They can find their direction from the position of the Sun by day and the stars by night. They can also detect changes in the Earth's magnetic field as they fly over it. This tells them whether they are flying north, south, east or west. Some birds find their way by smell.

**Q** Do animals live in families?

**A** Some animals live together in herds or flocks, but others live in small family groups. This is a family of tamarin monkeys (above). The older brothers and sisters carry and help groom the babies.

**Q** How do birds fly?

**A** These pictures (below) show a duck beating its wings once as it flies. The downstroke (left) lifts the bird up and propels it forward. On the upstroke (right) the feathers are opened to let air through.

# HUMAN BODY

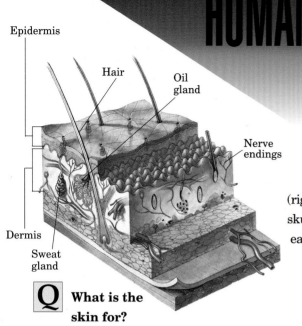

Epidermis

Hair

Oil gland

Nerve endings

Dermis

Sweat gland

**Q** What is the skin for?

**A** The skin (above) is the protective outer covering of our body. It contains nerve endings, which detect pain; sweat glands, which keep the body cool; and hair. It also prevents the body from losing too much water.

**Q** How do muscles work?

**A** There are more than 600 muscles in the body (right). Most of them move parts of the body or help it to stay upright. Muscles cannot push, they can only pull. Many of them work in pairs, attached to bones by tendons. One muscle tightens and becomes shorter, pulling the bone after it. If it relaxes, and the other muscle tightens, the bone moves back.

**Q** How many bones do we have?

**A** Humans have 206 bones in their bodies (right). There are 29 in the skull, 26 in the spine, 32 in each arm, and 31 in each leg. Other bones form the ribcage.

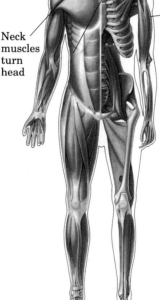

Chest muscles used in breathing

Neck muscles turn head

Tibia and Fibula (shin bones)

Upper arm muscles bend and straighten elbow

Sk

Collar bone

Ribca

Pelvis

Femur (thigh bone)

S

**Q** What is inside a bon

**A** Bones are not solid. They have a strong outer layer of compact bone, with lightweigh spongy bone inside. In the centr is the soft marrow, which makes new red cells for the blood.

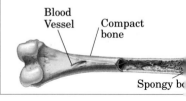

Blood Vessel

Compact bone

Spongy bo

**What are veins and arteries?**

When blood leaves the lungs, it carries oxygen. This blood travels [alo]ng vessels called arteries. The body [abs]orbs the oxygen, and the blood travels [bac]k to the heart through veins (below).

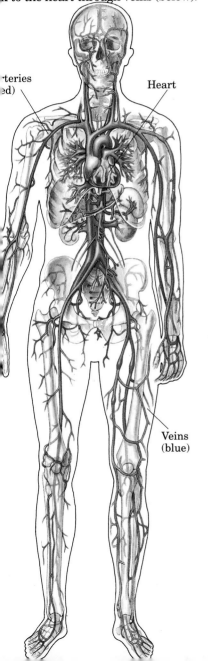

Right
atrium

Left
atrium

Left
ventricle

Right
ventricle

[Ar]teries
[(red)]

Heart

Veins
(blue)

**How does the heart work?**

The heart is a muscular pump. Oxygen-rich blood from the lungs enters the left side of the heart and is pumped to the organs. Veins carry the blood back to the right side of the heart. The blood is then pumped back to the lungs.

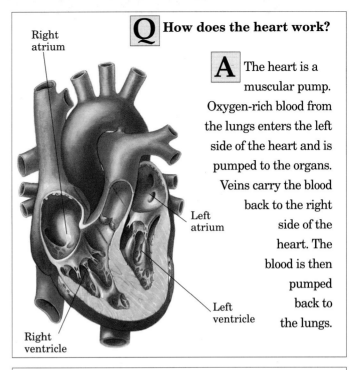

**How do our joints work?**

Joints are the places where bones move against each other. Shoulders and hips have ball and socket joints. These allow movement in any direction. Elbows have hinge joints, which allow them to move backwards and forwards. A pivot joint allows the head to turn sideways.

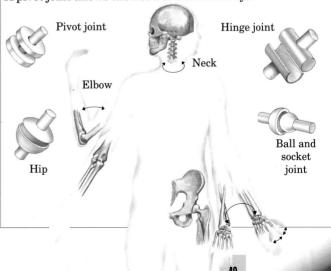

Pivot joint

Hinge joint

Neck

Elbow

Ball and
socket
joint

Hip

# SENSES & ORGANS

## Q How do we breathe?

**A** Our bodies need oxygen, which they get from air breathed into the lungs. The lungs are made to expand by a big muscle called the diaphragm, and smaller muscles fixed to the ribs. The diaphragm pushes downwards, while the other muscles lift up the rib cage. This draws air down into the lungs, where the oxygen is absorbed into the blood stream (right).

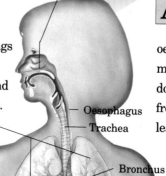

Air breathed in through nose and mouth

Lungs

Oesophagus

Trachea

Bronchus

Diaphragm

## Q Where does our food go?

**A** After the teeth chew the food, it is swallowed and goes down the oesophagus into the stomach (below). It is mixed with digestive juices, which break it down. In the small intestine, nutrients from the food are absorbed. Waste matter leaves the body through the anus.

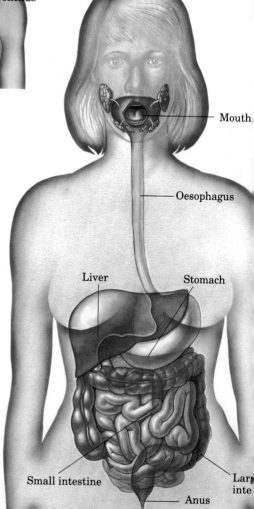

Mouth

Oesophagus

Liver

Stomach

Small intestine

Large intestine

Anus

## Q How do our eyes see?

**A** When we look at something, light from it enters our eyes. The light is focused on the retina at the back of the eye by the lens. The optic nerves in the retina send a message to the brain, enabling us to 'see'.

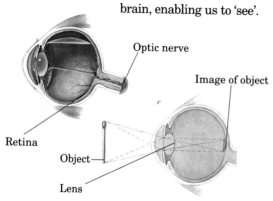

Optic nerve

Image of object

Retina

Object

Lens

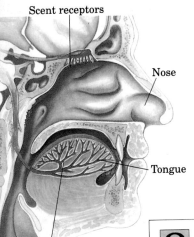

Scent receptors

Nose

Tongue

Taste receptors

## Q How do we taste and smell?

A In the upper part of the nose are tiny scent receptors (left). When we sniff, molecules in the air are carried to these receptors. They sense what we are smelling. The tongue is covered with about 9,000 taste receptors, or taste buds. These sense what we are tasting. The taste buds are grouped in special areas on the tongue. Sweetness is tasted at the front, saltiness and sourness at the sides, and bitterness at the back.

## Q How do our ears work?

A The outer ear collects sound waves, which pass through the eardrum and vibrate the tiny bones in the middle ear. These vibrations set the fluid in the cochlea in motion, shaking tiny hairs. Nerves attached to the hairs pass the message to the brain.

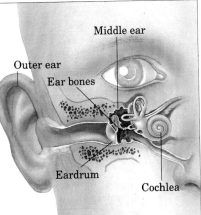

Middle ear

Outer ear

Ear bones

Eardrum

Cochlea

2 weeks

4 weeks

6 weeks

8 weeks

## Q How does a baby develop during pregnancy?

A A baby's life begins when a male sperm joins a female egg. The sperm travels from a man into a woman's body. It joins with the egg to form a single cell, and starts to grow. After a week, the single cell has multiplied to more than 100 cells. After eight weeks, the baby has all its major organs (such as heart, liver and lungs). The baby gets its food from its mother through the umbilical cord. After nine months, the baby is about 50 centimetres long (left). It is ready to be born.

Baby

Uterus

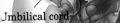

Umbilical cord

# INDEX